I0189215

IMAGES
of America

BELLAIRE

Business Section, Bellaire, Mich.

This aerial view of the village was taken just after the beginning of the 20th century. The new 1905 courthouse, without the clock yet, is clearly seen as well as the bank building, Kearney Township Hall, and the Waldmere Hotel on the east side of Bridge Street. Flye Hardware is on the corner opposite the town hall. The road east out of town is now Stover Road. (Courtesy of the Bellaire Area Historical Society.)

ON THE COVER: This is the first known picture of the Bellaire House, which was the first and only hotel in Keno (Bellaire) when it became the Antrim County seat of government in 1879. The hotel was built by John E. Cook using lumber from the Ferrand Mill. The building material was delivered on stone boats, as wheeled transportation was impossible due to the condition of the surrounding grounds. (Courtesy of the Bellaire Area Historical Society.)

IMAGES
of America

BELLAIRE

Bellaire Area Historical Society

ARCADIA
PUBLISHING

Copyright © 2010 by Bellaire Area Historical Society
ISBN 978-1-5316-3906-8

Published by Arcadia Publishing
Charleston SC, Chicago IL, Portsmouth NH, San Francisco CA

Library of Congress Control Number: 2009925359

For all general information contact Arcadia Publishing at:
Telephone 843-853-2070
Fax 843-853-0044
E-mail sales@arcadiapublishing.com
For customer service and orders:
Toll-Free 1-888-313-2665

Visit us on the Internet at www.arcadiapublishing.com

*This book is dedicated to the memory of those who
lived during this historical time and to those who
worked diligently to commemorate their lives.*

CONTENTS

ACKNOWLEDGMENTS

We in the 20th century are far removed from the lifestyles that carved Bellaire out of a dense and dangerous forest. For many of us the problems these pioneers faced would seem nearly impossible to overcome. Yet they persevered, and in the process they built a future for those now living in and visiting this pleasant town on the Intermediate River.

Unfortunately, identifying every source for the information and photographs in this book is an almost impossible task, because for a long period of time, many individuals and families anonymously donated pictures, letters, and memoirs to the Bellaire Area Historical Society. In addition, audio clips of early settlers' recollections were recorded by Bellaire Area Historical Society members and friends who were not identified on the tapes.

Unless otherwise noted, all images appear courtesy of the Bellaire Area Historical Society. Sources of information for individuals and families are either the subjects themselves, through writings and audiotapes, or provided by unidentified descendents living in Bellaire.

The following publications were consulted: *Covered Wagon Saga* by Nellye Pendock Dunson, *Memories of Bellaire* by Minnie Pendock Wellman, and *Biographical History of Northern Michigan* collected by B. F. Bowman.

Society members and associates who researched and assembled this book include Betty Hoover, Beverly Johnson, Marian Hill, Barbara Somerville, and Marjorie Fleet, all of whom consider this truly a "labor of love."

INTRODUCTION

The forests, lakes, and rivers of Bellaire have attracted people to the area since the first Native Americans made their homes along these waterways in and around the current town. The dense forests provided the materials necessary for building, cooking, and keeping warm in the northern Michigan winters.

In the 19th century, several factors lured people of European ancestry to the town site. The woods were an economic windfall in the late 1800s when the nation was spreading out after the fractures of the Civil War and needed lumber for booming construction as well as for heat. Effects of the War Between the States were evident in the number of Civil War veterans who came to this location to start new lives—some single and others with entire families. Many farmed the acres they were awarded for their service in the war. Antrim County, with its numerous lakes and rivers, was well suited for transporting tree trunks to the mills and was among many areas booming with lumbering, sawmills, and new construction. In fact, more money was made by lumbering the northern woods of Michigan and transporting it throughout the states than was made in the California Gold Rush of that era.

Naturally, villages sprang up where they were most convenient for lumber mills. In time, Antrim County had communities scattered throughout the entire county, undertaking a variety of occupations. Quarters for the county government were housed in Elk Rapids on the Lake Michigan shore; however, as scattered settlements grew larger around the county, the need for a more central location for conducting county business became more and more necessary to alleviate traveling long distances. Members of the outlying communities found it extremely difficult to travel through the countryside with the few roads that were no more than trails through the dense forest. To attend to county matters in Elk Rapids took several days and drew them away from their homes and businesses.

The most centrally located site was a small settlement on the Intermediate River that bisected the county. Sometimes known as Intermediate Rapids, the place called Keno already had its own post office and a few businesses. Debates over efforts to move the county offices to the central location resulted in an April 1879 election that approved the move 574 to 446.

Following the vote, the courthouse square was selected on a piece of land owned by Ambrose Palmer in the heart of the Keno settlement, yet the political climate was not totally in favor of the move. A lawsuit was brought against the county treasurer who refused to pay the bills involving any costs of moving the county seat. The case finally found its way to the Michigan State Supreme Court, with a settlement in favor of the Keno site made on June 9, 1880.

When the new town was renamed Bellaire shortly after completion of the court case, a large group of residents and visitors held a celebration by inflating balloons, painting them with the name Keno, and sending them off into the skies as a farewell to the old settlement and a celebration of the new village. It is said that the new name commemorated the high quality of the fresh and clean air around the village.

The next 20 years saw Bellaire grow by leaps and bounds, and by the 1900 census, the village limits supported about 1,200 people. Many of these settlers came from out of state or from foreign countries. By the early decades of the 20th century, the village offered four grocery stores, four dry goods stores, four hardware stores, two drugstores, two variety stores, five saloons and poolrooms, a bowling alley, three large hotels, two blacksmiths, a large opera house, four churches, eight doctors, two dentists, a jeweler, two newspapers, a bakery, two livery stables, a furniture and undertaking parlor, six lumber mills, a school with kindergarten through 12th grade, five meat markets, three shoe and harness shops, seven barbershops, a bank, telephone and telegraph offices, daily passenger and freight trains, two boat services a day between Bellaire and Elk Rapids, a tailor shop, two millineries, and two photograph studios as well as the Antrim County Courthouse and Jail.

Leisure time in those early years was generally family oriented or consisted of gatherings with friends in their homes. Children and adults loved popping corn, pulling taffy, playing cards, board games and activity games, reading aloud, and leading songfests. In addition, the town supported a host of other diversions. Among them were traveling shows at the opera house (the Kearney Township Hall), movies at the theater, public dances on all holidays, huge Fourth of July celebrations, Sunday rides on the rivers and lakes, swimming, an indoor roller-skating rink, outdoor ice-skating and sledding, and high school and adult baseball and basketball games. Youth and adults of all ages loved fishing, not only for food on the table, which was an essential need, but also for recreation.

Developing a viable school system was a top priority among the very early settlers. Many one-room schoolhouses dotted the countryside around Bellaire. Teachers were young, unmarried women who had graduated from normal schools that taught a nine-month course centered on educational techniques. For children living in town, classes were held in a single schoolhouse a few blocks north of the downtown area. Before long they had to expand into a two-room school, and soon they were holding classes in the Forest Home Hall. With diligence and hard work, the citizens raised money for a two-story brick school building that, within a few years, had to be doubled in size. As some of the country children reached their early teens, efforts were made to get them into the high school for as long as possible. One way this was accomplished was for the teens to spend the winter in the village homes of friends or relatives. Bellaire residents continue to value the importance of education and currently have two separate school buildings, an elementary school and a middle school/high school.

Bellaire enjoyed its 100th birthday in 1979 with a week of various activities and a grand parade. In 2009, the village was 130 years old. This historical account limits itself to the stories of its early settlements through the 1930s. Many of the families who were part of the hustle and bustle of Bellaire's early years still have descendents living there in the 20th century, enjoying the life their ancestors worked so hard to provide.

This volume focuses on the first 60 years of development within the village, ending in 1940 just before the United States entered World War II. It is hoped that another generation of local citizens will do the same for the next 60 years following that war.

One

THE EARLY FAMILIES

The last of the original Native American residents living around Bellaire, Peter Mark lived to be over 100 years old. He enjoyed regaling local children with the story of a fierce battle near Lake Bellaire and the Grass River between the Ottawa and Chippewa tribes, who were the original residents in that area, over a "pot of gold." Mark was a familiar sight in the village until his death in the early 1900s.

Roswell Leavitt earned his law degree from the University of Michigan and came to Bellaire in 1879 when Antrim County voted to move the county seat from Elk Rapids to Bellaire; however, the issue was not yet settled. A dispute with county treasurer R. W. Bagot over payment of bills escalated into a lawsuit brought before the Michigan State Supreme Court. County prosecutor Leavitt represented the board of supervisors against Bagot who questioned the validity of the vote. Judge Thomas Cooley found in favor of the board, and Bagot resigned. In 1881, Leavitt built the Inter-Lake House hotel in Bellaire. He also served a term as state senator.

In 1872, George and Jane Sackett Vandemark homesteaded in Antrim County, west of the settlement on the Intermediate River. According to granddaughter Hattie Hill Hope, they attended the 1879 event naming Bellaire as the county seat when organizers inflated balloons with the former name "Keno" printed on them and released them into the sky to carry the old name away. Wolves still roamed the woods at the Vandemark homestead, and during the summer, the family put torches in the open windows at night so the wolves would not enter their home.

Robert Richardi and his wife, Louise, moved to Bellaire around 1879. He and Frederick Bechtold constructed a dam on the Intermediate River and built the Richardi and Bechtold Woodenware Company factory. They achieved national fame at the 1893 World's Columbian Exposition in Chicago, winning first place for the greatest variety of products and second place for excellent workmanship. Shortly after, Bechtold left to found the Bellaire State Bank.

Early settlers Harry Reiley and Nora Brink Reiley (seated at center) were married October 5, 1885. They owned a large farm where they brought up their family of nine children: Willgert, Marnie, Millie, Cassie, Lena, Lulu, Charles, Harry, and Nora. Millie (back row with black bow) married Benjamin Arthur Powell, and they made their home on Durham Street in Bellaire. (Courtesy of Marion Reiley Seidenstucker.)

Pictured from left to right are Gertrude Jones Richardi with her husband, Henry, and two unidentified friends at the Grand Canyon They married in 1918. Henry sold his business interests in Michigan, and they moved to California. (Courtesy of Ken Fedraw.)

Publisher and owner of the *Bellaire Independent* newspaper, Ira A. Adams (in gray suit) printed his first issue on June 20, 1895, and the last issue on December 26, 1919. He bought the Bellaire House hotel in 1901 and also owned a dry goods store next door. He held the offices of county treasurer, county clerk, and register of deeds. From 1901 to 1912, he was president of the very popular Bellaire men's baseball team.

Civil War veteran Frederick W. Bechtold came to Bellaire to partner with Robert Richardi in their jointly named Richardi and Bechtold Woodenware Company. Then in August 1906, he and a board of directors began the Bellaire State Bank. The first president of the village in 1879, he served on the school board when the brick schoolhouse was built. He and his wife, Maximiliana, made their home on Park Street, where they raised 13 children.

Nellye Pendock Dunson's grandfather, Thomas Kiser, left his Ohio farm with his wife, Catherine, and seven children to travel 425 miles north in a covered wagon. When they arrived in Bellaire on October 18, 1879, they camped overnight on Bridge Street and trekked to their homestead the next day. Their daughter Renie (second row, center) married, and the couple moved to Bellaire where Nellye was raised.

William J. Nixon moved to Bellaire in 1880 with experience working in a dry goods store in Chicago and opened a general store with his brother Allen. He married Emma Louisa Richardi in 1883, and the home on Park Street where they raised their children is now the Bellaire Bed and Breakfast. The couple owned the Nixon Grocery in one of the first brick buildings erected downtown on Bridge Street.

Clark Densmore moved to Bellaire in the early 1880s to establish his legal practice, and in 1886, he married Harriet Dawson of Central Lake. Densmore was elected county clerk in 1902. He also served as president of Bellaire, as county prosecutor, and on the board of education. He and Harriet held membership in the United Methodist Church, the Masonic Lodge, and the Eastern Stars and raised seven children.

William and Maggie Hierlihy arrived in Bellaire in 1896. There William began business as an apprentice shoemaker. By 1900, he had his own leather business on Bridge Street, where he invented the Never Slip Heel Plates that prevented slipping on ice. They gained national attention when Adm. Richard E. Byrd used them on the Antarctic Expedition. William secured WPA funds to build the current Bellaire Community Hall. (Courtesy of Bud Hierlihy.)

Theodore N. Chapin moved to Bellaire from Kent County in 1883 and married Vesta J. Hutchinson. He won the office of Antrim County sheriff, serving from 1911 to 1914, and ran for the Michigan House of Representatives, where he represented Antrim County for three terms, from 1915 to 1921. The family raised milk cows and tended fruit orchards on their 200-acre farm.

Bellaire native Neil A. Alcott, born in 1883, was well known for his landscaping and gardening talents. During the spring and summer, his horticultural skills were in great demand throughout the growing season. In three different years, he was awarded status as a plant grower and buyer by the Michigan Department of Agriculture, authorizing him to grow and sell the plants and flowers nurtured in his Alcott's Dream Garden.

16

Arriving in Bellaire in 1887, Harvey M. Hemstreet was an associate in the grocery business on Bridge Street. He served terms as justice of the peace and as coroner for Antrim County. In addition, he served as treasurer for Forest Home Township and another time for the Village of Bellaire. He and his wife, Harriet, grew apples, pears, cherries, peaches, and plums in their orchards northwest of town. (Courtesy of Caren Culver.)

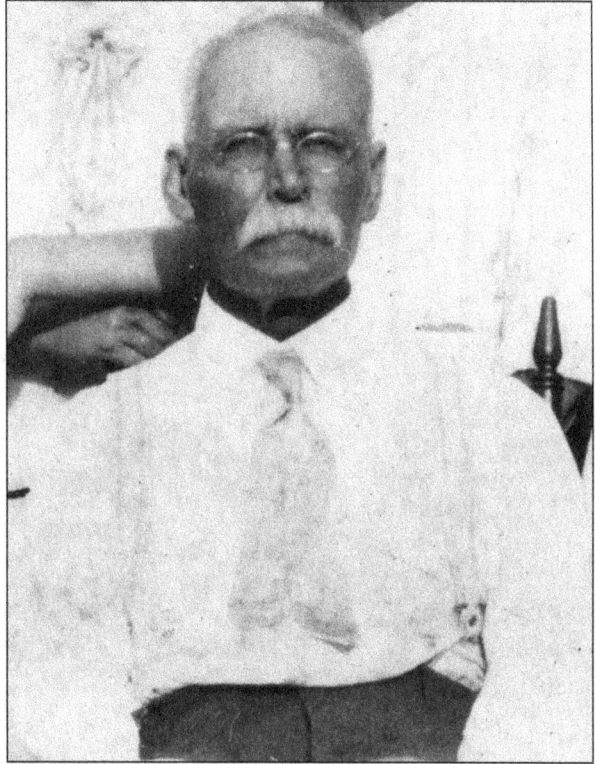

Frank Wilks and Lilly Besaw, both born in Antrim County, married in 1899 and made their home on the northwest corner of East Cayuga and Depot Streets, where they raised 12 children. Frank's blacksmith shop was on the corner of Bridge and Cayuga Streets, and Lilly's family owned a shop downtown. Wilks's large garden supplied flowers and produce for family and friends. The couple celebrated their golden anniversary in 1949. (Courtesy of Marlene Hardy.)

According to Minnie Pendock Wellman (pictured here), her mother, Hattie Thayer Pendock, born in 1859, was the first white child born in Antrim County, the daughter of Lucius and Helen Thayer. Minnie spent her early years at home on the south arm of Lake Bellaire. In January 1895, when she was four, her family decided to move into Bellaire. With no roads leading to town, the frozen lake provided a hard-surface freeway for the move. The sleigh her father used was loaded with all their household goods and clothing. It looked just like a covered wagon with runners instead of wheels. They climbed the hill below the cemetery to the road west of town. To make the final mile into town, her father and brothers had to stop the wagon many times and shovel snow for several feet so the oxen could pull the sleigh into town. The Wellman home, where she raised her family, was just across the road from the high school parking lot. She was widely known for her exquisite iris gardens and won horticultural awards for them.

Two

LOGS AND RAILS

Logging the forests was one of the major motivations for laying railroads to Bellaire. Though logs were moved out of the woods by real horsepower, transporting the finished timber products was best accomplished by using the steam power of railroads. The "wooden gold" from Bellaire fueled construction throughout the Midwest and beyond.

Winter was always the best time to move logs to the mills in town. Teams of horses could drag sleds of logs more easily in the snow than on bare ground. Working at this camp north of Bellaire were, from left to right, Matt Borwick, Col Borwick, Ed Schwab, and two other unidentified men.

Logging required a great deal of manpower and horsepower. These loggers included Jerry Bedell, George Bedell, Gerald Bedell, Russell Thomas, Ernest McIntyre, Clinton Thomas, Robert Shirea, William Thomas, Robert Oxby, H. A. Thomas, Ozzie McIntyre, and Allen Thomas. Long rods had big hooks used for piling the logs in stacks.

In many instances, logging camps included women and sometimes children. The women may have been the loggers' wives working and staying with their husbands, while sisters, daughters, and friends may have only stayed there during the day. Either way, they lived the same rugged lives and faced many of the same dangers as the men. They were responsible for cooking the meals, cleaning the cabins, and keeping the clothes clean. In some cases, they carried weapons and killed the meat needed by the hardworking men. With the men away in the forests all day, the women cleaned and butchered the animals as well as cooked and served the meat.

Family day at the logging camp was the perfect day for a photographer to record the gathering. While this is a great picture, unfortunately the families have not been identified.

Early lumber camps used oxen as well as horses for hauling the timber. The stories of these workingmen and their animals gave rise to such tales as those of Paul Bunyan and Babe the Blue Ox. In some cases, the men working the woods used their own stock to pull the heavy sleighs full of logs.

At the start of the work, these six men—from left to right, Frank Parks, Fred Hood, unidentified man, Fred Covert, Gerald Bedell, and Archie Priest—pause for a moment for this photograph. Their equipment is sparse, as they get the better of the trees with their axes and horses. Many men were local residents, while others followed the work from camp to camp.

Before the teams of horses or oxen arrived to haul logs away, the lumbermen had to pile the logs in one place for better loading. Logging west of Bellaire in 1893 were, from left to right, Otto Richardi (cousin to Henry Richardi), Nate Thayer (in the background), Eli Thayer, Joe Feree, Will Thayer Jr., and an unidentified worker holding the hook they used to make the piles.

Men working long hours far from camp liked to use their lunch hour to relax and amuse themselves. These two "sparring partners" entertain their fellow loggers in a fisticuffs game. Some of the men watching hold their own axes. Most loggers were accustomed to the heft of their axes and knew the best way to sharpen their own blades.

It might not be noticeable at a casual glance, but tree bark is loaded with sand and other material blown by the wind. This makes it more difficult for the saw to slice through, requiring many work stops to sharpen blades. Roy Wolcott (left) and his unidentified partner notched the tree with axes before putting the crosscut saw to work.

Whatever supplies were needed while out logging, especially lunch, had to be taken with the loggers when they left camp for the woods. These loggers take time out for their noon meal and a chance to sit for a while. They always made sure their horses were well fed and watered as well.

At least three men handle these logs being floated through town on the Intermediate River under the Bridge Street Bridge. They may be heading for the Warner Sawmill on the river at the Warner Bridge west of downtown. In the background, the Riverside Hotel stands on the south bank of the river.

Hosmer's Mill was situated in the village of Bellaire on the Cedar River north of Broad Street, just before the river drains into the Intermediate River. Among the men in this photograph taken in 1916 are, from left to right, Charles Smith, another Mr. Smith, Bill Russel, Clyde Green, Frank Martin, Neil Alcott, Charles Lutz, Cyrus Glass, Will Cotton, Fred Miles, and Luther Markley.

Several mills in and around Bellaire processed the logs brought in from the surrounding woods. Numerous workers and their animals spent long hours bringing raw materials into the local mills, then transporting finished lumber to local factories and train yards for transportation to many cities. Logs and finished lumber drove the local economy for about 40 years.

The Tindle and Jackson hoop and stave mill in Bellaire provided employment for at least 24 men. The January 2, 1902, edition of the *Bellaire Independent* featured a large front-page article describing the firm's success at the Pan-American Exposition in Buffalo, New York: "Received the Highest Award." The selection of goods manufactured in Bellaire mills by Tindle and Jackson was recognition of Antrim County timber and its expert, careful workmen.

At the turn of the 20th century, the woods became noisier with the invention of a new contraption that was able to haul several sleds at one time: The front appears to be a snowmobile with runners and a light, while behind it, the steam engine looks like a train engine on tracks instead of rails.

For housing, crews laying railroads lived in railcars always at the job site. A kitchen and dining car, sleeping cars with bunk beds, and a car for handling the accounting books and other business met all their needs. Railroads employed mainly immigrants instead of local men, and they worked the whole line.

The Pere Marquette Depot, built in 1892, bustled with activity as passenger and freight trains ran north and south through town several times each day. Some arrived to pick up travelers, while other onlookers came just to watch the hustle and bustle, especially when freight trains were changing cars—leaving some and taking others.

Several men stand alongside the depot in this early-20th-century photograph. The horses and wagon behind them belong to the Maltby Barn on Broad Street. On a daily basis, the Maltbys ran back and forth from the station delivering the mail to the post office and goods to downtown stores, businesses, and hotels.

On rare occasions a train wreck occurred, drawing crowds of onlookers. This train engine ran into a flatcar, separating the frame from the wheels without apparent injury to the crew or passengers. Travelers from the passenger train left their car to assess the damage that halted their trip until other arrangements could be made.

The train tracks ran north and south along the east side of what is now Depot Street. In this photograph, two men stand at the intersection where the rails cross Cayuga Street. The rails were abandoned in the late 1970s, and the main railroad bed is now a very popular walking path through town.

The Pere Marquette engine No. 157, with the engineer standing on the cab steps, stopped for this photograph with some of the passengers who were either boarding for a trip north or arriving from the south in the early 1900s. Heavy wagon-wheel tracks in the foreground attest to the numerous loads taken to and from the train.

Heavy winter snow was a constant concern along the rails, but it seldom prevented the trains from keeping close to their schedule. As this train huffs its way north, passengers who just disembarked walk along Broad Street toward downtown. Some are returning home, while others have business to conduct in Bellaire.

Three

EDUCATION AND SCHOOLS

Built among forest trees, Bellaire's first school, in use by 1881, was located on the northwest corner of Bridge and Hastings Streets. The entrance hall leading into the single classroom held several large shelves for coats, a water pail with dipper, and a mirror on the wall with a comb on a string hung by a nail. Before long, a second student room was added. (Painting by Marian Hill.)

The new school site on Forest Home Avenue, where the current high school is now located, was purchased from Roswell Leavitt in December 1888. The two-story structure accommodated all the grades. It faced south along the north side of the avenue, two blocks from Bridge Street. In 1890, the first year in this building, only two classrooms were finished, but soon the others were ready to be occupied.

During a special meeting held on April 13, 1908, the school board voted to spend $12,000 for an addition that doubled the size of the school building. Elementary grades took up the original portion (left) with the high school housed in the new construction (right). In addition to the children living in the village, students from the surrounding country schools enrolled in the high school.

235

BELLAIRE, MICH. KINDERGARTEN

Not too many years passed before the small school added a second room to accommodate the increase in village children attending elementary grades. Even that was not enough, and more classes were held in the Forest Home Township Hall, situated where the present hall is located on Bridge Street. A kindergarten class of 29 students (above) and a second grade class of 22 students (below) posed on the front porch of the Richardi House to commemorate their school year. By 1889, school enrollment had increased so rapidly the board raised $7,000 to construct a completely new building.

Pupils in this first-grade class from around 1919 posing on the steps are, from left to right, (first row) Annabelle Lee, Margaret Harvey, Della Nichols, Josephine Densmore, and Genevieve Hilton; (second row) Mildred Slingerland, Irene Smith, Clara Wilson, Irma Wilks, Julia Waite, and Elizabeth Fuller; (third row) teacher Miss Shattuck, Leon Biladeau, Vernon Wilks, Harold "Pete" Sexton, Floyd McPherson, and Irwin Clapp.

Among the third graders seated at their desks were Robert Allen, Hazel Brown, Milo Smith, Beatrice Smith, Alta Harper, Vivian Seamen, Fred Muckey, Violet Seaman, Eddie Childs, and Gerald Shetrom. The shades were drawn on the lower parts of the windows whenever the sun hit the corner classroom.

Often two classes were taught by one teacher. Mrs. Reed (standing, far right) taught this fourth-and fifth-grade class around 1917. Although not all students are identified, some of the class members were William Richards, Doris Nickles, Bertha Hepburn, Alta Besaw, Lawrence Ritt, Edwin Williamson, Donna Hosmer, Arletta Reed, Bessie Kauphman, Hilda Dunn, Livisia Hicocks, George Sanford, and Erma Childs.

Bellaire School
Some of the students — Gwendolyn Large
Martha Finney, Earnest Schoolcraft
Clifford Lee, Herbie Walker, Marie Adams
Esther Goldstick, Nina Harper

The new school rooms in the elementary wing provided wall space for students to display their current work for all to see. Among those in this grade are Gwendolyn Large, Martha Finney, Earnest Schoolcraft, Clifford Lee, Herbie Walker, Marie Adams, Esther Goldstick, and Nina Harper. Artwork on the back wall includes paintings of autumn leaves and other scenes.

Classes continued to be taught in pairs as the 1890s turned into the 1900s. A group of fifth- and sixth-graders (above) gathered with their teachers who are at left in the upper row. All but two of the boys are wearing hats in the styles each one favored. Some wore knickers, and others chose full trousers. Large hair bows were the preference for some of the girls, and many of them wore white. The seventh- and eighth-grade students (below) also present a variety of styles. Bows in the girls' hair became bigger, and some of the boys wore ties with or without jackets. Math, reading, writing, science, and history were the core subjects for all the elementary grades.

High school superintendent H. L. Reynolds (fourth row above, with moustache and glasses) appears with the high school class on the front porch of the new school building completed in 1890. The students' attire was fairly formal around this time. The girls all wore long-sleeved dresses, many of them dark colors. All the boys wore suits, some with vests and ties and others with just the coat and pants. By 1916 (below), all the high school classes numbered nearly 100 students. Two of the instructors are standing at the far right in this group. By this time, many of the students came from the rural schoolhouses that dotted the countryside around Bellaire. They often boarded with village families during the winter so that they could complete their education.

School dress became more comfortable as the 20th century progressed. Members of this class are, from left to right, (first row) Phyllis Smith, Betty Wallays, five unidentified, Carl Alspaugh, and unidentified; (second row) Karin Fate, Max Clyde, Emogean Gregory, Junior Knutson, Jackie Burnett, Mary Lou Severance, Laura Belle Burnett, Dean Ousterhout, Margaret Wallays, and Betty Ingersoll; (third row) Bill Eggleston, Bob Phillips, teacher Mrs. McCulloch, two unidentified, June Steiner, three unidentified, and Dorr Mason.

As the school curriculum expanded, music was always popular with many students. Members of the 1932 school band gathered in front of the school are, from left to right, (first row) Ivan Steiner, Eloise Cook, Don Gorham, Don Wilson, Margaret Phillips, Etta Brundges, Darlo Gregory, and teacher Irma Richards; (second row) Virgil Thayer, James Bedell, and Victor Evans. Note the proper stance the students held with their instruments.

Playing in team sports gave high school students a break from book work, and these young ladies from the 1911 girls' basketball team took advantage of the opportunity. Not all of the players or the coach were identified in this photograph; however, the three young ladies in the third row are, from left to right, Grace Pickard, Marie Weiffenbach, and Jean Densmore. Two of the other players are Lillian Patterson and Grace Lee.

Members of the early sports teams usually played throughout the whole game. Team rosters were not very large, as many students were busy at their parents' businesses and farms. The 1913 Bellaire High School boys' basketball players are, from left to right, (first row) Shirley Mosher, Clifford Breidenstein, and Herbert Montague; (second row) Lewellyn Mayne, Elmer Fate, and coach/referee Mr. Brown.

By 1913, the girls' basketball team dress became a little looser, perhaps to allow for more freedom of movement. Players for the high school in 1914 were, from left to right in their new uniforms, (first row) Eva Flannagin and Dorothy Mayne; (second row) Marie Foster, Lillian Dewey, and Onabelle Millard; (third row) coach Leah Finkenauer and Olive Foster.

```
BELLAIRE BASKETBALL TEAM   1913 or 1914
```

```
Top Row (L to R)-- Miss Leah Finkenauer
                      (Stillwell) - Coach,
                  Olive Foster (Alsbaugh)
2nd Row-- Marie Foster, Lillian Dewey (Kauffman)
         Onabelle Millard
1st Row-- Eva Flannagin & Dorothy Mayne
```

Different uniforms and a sixth player made up the boys' basketball team around 1914 or 1915. New team members joined with some of the previous boys. Players in this senior high school team include, in no particular order, Clifford Breidenstein, Herbert Bechtold, Shirley Mosher, Lewellyn Mayne, Arthur Ward, and Floyd Mosher.

Members of the Bellaire High School girls' basketball team in 1924 wore their team sweaters and long black stockings for this photograph. Not all the names of the players are known for this picture, but among this group of eight hoopsters are Erma Childs, Avis Morrow, Lillian Sexton, and Helen Fitzpatrick.

By 1937, the boys' basketball team expanded to a dozen members. Playing hoops for Bellaire were, from left to right, (first row) Milton Richards, Charles Bush, Jacob Watrous, Wayne Steiner, Perry Mills, and Daryl Ward; (second row) William Sexton, George Gardner, Carlton Dunson, principal/coach John Schuring, Richard Wilks, Hugh Mosher, and Bruce Brown.

The 1895 senior class graduating from Bellaire High School included, from left to right, (first row) valedictorian Emma Cutler; (second row) salutatorian Edgar Wilcox, W. Burgess May, L. Frank Cleveland, Clyde Leavitt, and George M. Gorham. The very first graduates in 1894 were five young men: Lewis E. Stewart, Arch M. Eldred, Samuel B. Abbott, Alfred A. Hickox, and Samuel W. Large. Graduation was held in the Kearney Township Hall for some time.

Graduating classes of Bellaire High School remained relatively small through the first few years. Again, only one girl—Rosetta Weiffenbach—graduated in 1902. The young men were Hayward Noteware, Earl Wellman, Fred Bechtold, and Ray Wellman. Their families and friends filled the Methodist Church with the largest crowd ever assembled in that building, with even standing room at a premium.

By 1908, the graduating class size had grown. Members of this class and their sobriquets were "popular" president Ford Densmore, "smiling" Alida Dearborn, "agreeable, languid" Opal Montague, "one to meet" Abbie Shetron, "deacon" George Petrie, "human volcano" Norma May, "always sunny" Ethel Densmore, "quiet and gentle" Sadie Perry, "best pitcher" George Bechtold, "pious critic" Grace Gardner, "aggravates the soil" Jennie Breidenstein, "golden-haired" Charlotte Adamson, and "Polly" Charlie Cross.

The graduating class of 1909 was one of the largest of that era, and many of the students would have been together since kindergarten. Class members were, in alphabetical order, Zula Adams, Rudolph Bechtold, Zora Chapin, Arlie Childs, Alice Coldren, Shirley Densmore, Clyde Dewey, Lyle Dickerson, Lee Farrell, Willie Maltby, Claude Matthews, Lenore Nixon, Irl Noteware, Ray Owen, Allen Petrie, Will Phelps, Millie Reiley, Helena Weiffenbach, and Charles Wellman.

By 1921, the size of the graduating classes had grown much larger. This class of 17 students included, from left to right, (first row) Royal Akins, Essie Friend, Margaret Chambers, and Edgar Bacon; (second row) teacher Ellen Crawford, Walter Crandall, Doris Bedell, superintendent R. J. Sisson, Alta Harper, Paul Akins, and teacher Ellen Taggart; (third row) Maud Wilson, Ethel Stonehouse, Merle Wilson, Iveron Hill, Luella Hemstreet, Nellie Densmore, and teacher Gertrude Phillip.

Graduates in 1923 were (first row, seated) Bertha Smith, Shirley Underhill, Neva Manuel, Edith Stonehouse, superintendent R. J. Sisson, Ula Butler in front of Melva Thompson, Elda Dewey in front of Leola Manuel, and Irene Bruce; (second row) Helen Dewey, Norval Smith, teacher Anah Smith, Orlie Washburn, teacher Ellen Crawford, Roy Blakesley, Wilma Gardner, King Smith, and Leora Robinson; (third row) teacher Ezra Devereau, Erma Washburn, Jack Harvey, Dorothy Downing, Lawrence Crandall, Frances Bucy, and two unidentified.

Fifteen seniors graduated in the class of 1927. They are, from left to right, (first row) superintendent Frank Davis, Marian Thomas, Nettie Pataniczek, and Fred Price; (second row) Ina Patton, Fred Gervers, teacher Mable Olson, Dora Hill, Durward Wellman, teacher Anah Bechtold, Clair Cook, and Arthur Irwin; (third row) Orley Crandall, Robert Jewell, Adrien Anderson, Mary Downing, principal Edward Heyman, Anna Jager, Leroy Beal, and teacher Orrin Lathrop.

The 1928 graduating seniors and their instructors were, from left to right, (first row) Jean Heath, Aethale Smith, Marie Berg, Durah Hepburn, Vivian Richards, Nora Thomas, and Arlie Bedell; (second row) George Palmer, Mable Montgomery, Alice Underhill, George Richards, Erma Watrous, Hoy Dewey, Carrie Manuel, and Leroy Bruce; (third row) teacher Esther Bliton, teacher Orrin Lathrop, Iva Orcutt, Steve Shippy, teacher Mabel Olson, superintendent Ed Heyman, Gladys Derenzy, and Gerald Green.

The graduating class of 1930 posing for this picture is, from left to right, (first row) Esther Laven, Eunice Butler, Avis Dingman, Dwight Mills, Rachel Greenman, Elizabeth Fuller, and Fern Steiner; (second row) teacher Miss Schail, Vernon Butler, teacher Vida Casey, Dorval Simpson, Ruth Wilson, VernonWilks, and Genevieve Hilton; (third row) Lowell Watrous, Emily Austin, "Bizz" Montague, principal Mr. VanPatten, teacher Mr. Anderson, Bernice Hilton, and Robert Hinman.

Gathered on the front lawn, the 1931 junior and senior class is, from left to right, (first row) Eugene Bruce, Frank Tyler, Leo Berg, Harry Steiner, and Herrick Baker; (second row) Flora Watrous, Lucille Green, Madeline Hierlihy, Florence Morrow, Freda Mohrman, Mildred Bedell, Laura Weeman, Dannie Junker, Donald Richards, and Cody Pelham; (third row) Esther Montgomery, Carol Smith, Pearl Sheneman, Glen Dingman, senior class advisor Mr. Anderson, junior class adviser Mr. VanPelten, George Sigler, Alice Bedell, Mildred Watrous, and Homer Schuler.

Four

A PICTORIAL WALK

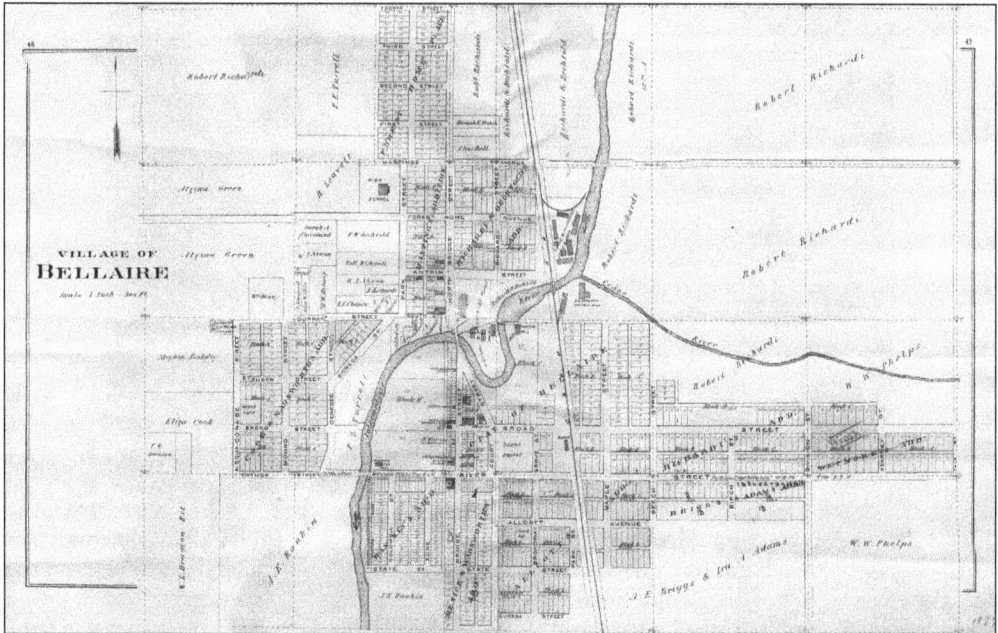

This is a pictorial walk through the village of Bellaire, beginning with Keno in 1879 through Bellaire in 1940 and from Grass Lake to Lake Bellaire. The village plat of 1879 clearly shows that the city's early planners believed in an unending expansion of the area.

First M.E.Church,Bellaire,Mich.
Pub. by White's Bazaar.

The First Methodist Episcopal Church was dedicated on December 25, 1887. Prior to this, the small congregation held services in private homes and the schoolhouse. In 1885, two lots were purchased for a church building. The congregation raised $200 and borrowed $2,000 from the Board of Church Extension of Philadelphia. The plans for the church were chosen from the "Catalogue of Architectural Plans for Churches and Parsonages." Local builder E. J. Childs was hired, and Robert Richardi furnished the surety bond. Stones for the foundation came from the Ben Powell farm west of the village. Several problems arose during construction but were resolved quickly, and the church was completed in 1887 with a dedication by Rev. George Sherman. The church bell was installed on April 30, 1901. Now known as the Bellaire Community United Methodist Church, the church has stood at the northwest corner of Bridge and Antrim Streets for over 100 years.

According to church records, the first Catholic church in Bellaire was located in Block A, lots 11–17, at the corner of Broad and Beech Streets on land purchased from Fletcher and Mary Turrell in 1877. Soon a mission church was erected and was served by the Franciscan fathers from their friary of St. Francis Xavier in Petoskey, Michigan. Church records list St. Luke's as a station church in 1897. In March 1906, the local paper reported that the new tower of the Catholic church was being built to 55 feet in height (measured to the top of the cross), and when finished the society was prepared to place a 500-pound bell in the belfry. The church was destroyed by fire in July 1921. After the fire, the lots were sold, and two lots were purchased on Cayuga Street. There a church was raised by using the dismantled Atwood church. Services were held there once a month for 16 years.

Located on the southwest corner of Antrim and Park Streets, the Congregational Church was organized in 1883 by Rev. Warren P. Wilcox and was officially certified June 23, 1884. Reverend Wilcox also founded the Congregational Church of Central Lake. He and his wife, Marion (Winchell), served 18 different congregations in Michigan. One of the frequent guest speakers at the Bellaire church was Prof. George C. Catton, president of Benzonia College and father of historian Bruce Catton. This *c.* 1893 photograph of a Sunday school picnic (below) identifies a few individuals of the congregation. In the second row, seventh from the left, is Marion Wilcox, and next to her is Henry Lott, the school principal. Also in the second row is Robert Duderstadt (the bearded man at far left), who was the principal woodcarver at the woodenware factory. In the fourth row, second and third from left, are Amos Underwood and William Wilcox (Reverend Wilcox's son).

Charles Weiffenbach, one of the earliest Bellaire merchants, had his grocery on the west side of Bridge Street. He also owned one of the earliest cottages on the east shore of Grass Lake. He gained statewide notoriety in 1901 and 1902 by suing the State of Michigan and winning the right to sell "oleomargarine." A couple of doors north of the grocery store was the first drugstore in the village, owned by George James Noteware and his brother Waldo. George continued the business until he sold it to Alpha Large in 1903. Pictured at right is George James Noteware (1859–1911). He served many terms on the Bellaire School Board. He also built a cottage on the east shore of Grass Lake and donated part of the property for a public park, now recognized as Noteware's Landing.

Bridge Street,
Looking North
from Court Street,
Bellaire, Mich.

Local merchant Fred D. Flye came to Bellaire in 1898 from Kalkaska, where he had managed the Freeman Woodenware Company. He purchased Antrim Hardware, which was located on the northwest corner of Bridge and Broad Streets, but in early 1901, the building burned to the ground. Flye immediately contracted for a new structure, and by August the foundation was in place for a two-story brick building. Completed by October, the upper floor was rented to Dr. Carlos Putt, dentist, and William G. Warner, photographer. As the owner of the hardware store (above), Flye had sold more than 35 farm machines in one year, and to celebrate, he arranged this photograph of the machines on Broad Street (below). Also, any buyer who came to get his machine before noon was treated to a banquet dinner at the Bellaire House hotel.

Just north of Flye Hardware was the local barbershop, which had many owners through the years. In 1912, William "Bill" Sampson (left) purchased the shop from William "Bill" Moore (right). A street sign outside the barbershop advertised "Baths—25¢" in addition to the traditional offering of shaves and haircuts. A loyal citizen of Bellaire, Sampson sponsored the Bellaire baseball team.

For the maternal side of the population there was always a millinery shop. In April 1897, Mrs. T. R. Dunson advertised a cordial invitation to all in the local newspaper "to see our goods and get prices." This 1905 photograph of a millinery shop shows manager Mrs. Harper and Ethel Carr. The shop was located about four doors north of the hardware store on Bridge Street.

The Bellaire House, on the southwest corner of Bridge and Broad Streets, was built in 1879 by John Cook, then sold to Arthur and Juliet Watkins in 1881. This photograph was taken after the Watkins added a 30-feet-by-60-feet addition to the hotel, as there was an increased demand for rooms once Bellaire had become the county seat. Anyone who had business with the government usually had to stay overnight. The building on the left was Ira Adams General Store, and on the right of the hotel was the fire tower containing the bell that was rung in the event of a fire to call for the volunteer firefighters. The tower also served as a place to dry the hose after it had been used.

The Bellaire House, Bellaire, Mich.

In 1901, Juliet Watkins sold the Bellaire House hotel to businessman Ira A. Adams. The hotel could accommodate 35 guests, but by 1902, this was not enough, so he opened the second floor of his adjacent general store to guests. He continually upgraded the building by adding electric lights, central heating, and plumbing. In 1904, he added a brick addition to the north side of the hotel. Built as an annex, it was outfitted to take care of the salesmen's needs, a great place to display their wares. Like many buildings in the village, it had many lives: showroom, print shop (Ira Adams business), and saloon. In 1906, the fire bell was installed on the roof of the annex. Later this stand-alone building became the Masonic Lodge. The hotel was gone by 1924.

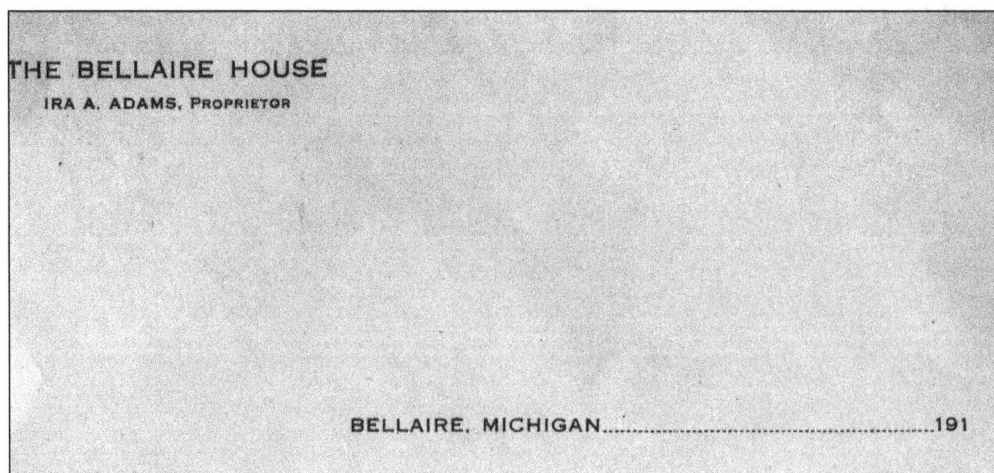

THE BELLAIRE HOUSE

IRA A. ADAMS, Proprietor

BELLAIRE, MICHIGAN...191

1910

⁕

The Bellaire House

A Happy New Year
to You

If a person could afford to eat out, he or she was surely well fed. This was a typical holiday menu.

Menu

Service from One to Two-Thirty O'clock

Celery   Queen Olives
                Oyster Cocktail
Clam Chowder   Salted Almonds

        Baked Fillet of Lake Trout a la Creole
Prime Roast Beef au Jus
        Baked Spring Chicken, Oyster Dressing
                        Spring Lamb, Caper Sauce
        Boiled Majestic Ham, Sliced Lemon

        Salmon Salad, French Dressing
Whipped Potatoes   Buttered Beets
        String Beans a la Chapelle

        Hot Baker's Rolls

Apple Pie, American Cheese   New England Mince Pie
                Pumpkin Pie
        Home-made English Plum Pudding, Wine Sauce
        Oranges   Figs   Mixed Nuts

Black and Green Tea   Milk   Coffee

Pictured is Bellaire's merchant tailor, August F. Banowske (1876–1965). He learned his trade as a tailor in his native Poland, apprenticing for a period of four years before purchasing his release two years later. His parents, David and Vena, had come to Bellaire at the request of Robert Richardi so David could work in his factory.

Banowske worked in other localities in Michigan, but in 1897, he opened a shop in Bellaire, and by 1898, he had built his own shop on the west side of Bridge Street. He served the community as a justice of the peace and in 1904 became the village treasurer and the clerk of Kearney Township. He also served as treasurer in the local camp of the Modern Woodmen of America. The message on the reverse side of this postcard, mailed by Banowske as advertising for his shop, claims that a "real merchant tailored suite" would cost $20 to $30 at other stores, but only $12 to $22 at the Worthmore Tailors Company. Banowske was so confident in his products and pricing that he even guaranteed customers, "You must be pleased or we won't take your money."

Special Novelty Model
Four-Button Sack
No. 277

Worthmore Models reflect the very newest style ideas. This is but one of forty-eight exclusive styles.

The Worthmore Tailors Company
CHICAGO

Banowske poses in shirtsleeves in front of his shop. The other gentleman is not identified. A cement sidewalk is evident, but the street is still unpaved. The shop was constructed in 1898 but destroyed in July 1921 by a devastating fire, which burned many buildings in the northerly part of the village. The crowds gathered the next day to view the burned areas.

63

This postcard depicts the opening of Banowske's safe—all that remained of his shop after the devastating fire.

PUBLIC PARK - BELLAIRE, MICH. 356-5.

The editor of the *Bellaire Independent* wrote, "[William] Hierlihy [merchant] and [John] Ticknor [harness salesman] have set a splendid example of civic pride in providing the neat little park on the vacant lots adjoining the farmer's place of business on Bridge Street. It's a private enterprise for the people's use, for which the citizens are very grateful. These public-spirited benefactors cannot be too highly commended." The park, constructed in June 1911 on the west side of Bridge Street between the Hierlihy building and the Nixon-Densmore building, was destroyed by vandals the following year.

Architect F. E. Moore and contractor A. E. Wilson arrived in Bellaire from Traverse City to make plans for the brick block of Clark E. Densmore and William J. Nixon on April 4, 1901. The double-front brick building with a central stairway to the upper floor was located on the west side of Bridge Street. The original Nixon Grocery Store was started by Nixon and his brother Bryan. In the right half was the general store, with the Independent Order of Odd Fellows Lodge occupying the second floor. The left half of the building was occupied by the Flanagin Brothers Dry Goods store. Densmore had offices in the front of the second floor, with Densmore Hall in the rear. In 1905, the hall was rented to the Latter-day Saints. In 1934, William's widow, Emma (Richardi), leased the Nixon Grocery Store to the state but continued to sell fresh vegetables from her home.

This is how the Densmore-Nixon block looked after the July 1921 fire. The brick wall stopped the flames from destroying many more buildings.

This photograph, dated 1895, shows the Hemstreet Brothers Groceries and Provisions store. The gentleman on crutches is Harvey M. Hemstreet (1840–1925), who lost his left leg when he was only seven years old. He and his brother Erwin (1851–1923) came to Bellaire and founded the store. In 1884, Harvey went to Nebraska to explore opportunities out west, but only stayed for three years. In the years between 1887 and 1899, they constructed a two-story brick building to house their grocery store. By 1899, Harvey sold his interest in the store to Erwin and devoted his full energy to his orchard farm. When Harvey sold his interest in the store, Erwin's son-in-law, Dr. Carlton Hinman, became a partner. In 1906, the partners sold the business to Horace L. Richards and his son James E. Richards.

In July 1906, Horace L. Richards (1852–1935) and his son James E. Richards purchased the Hemstreet and Hinman grocery store, a two-story brick structure on the east side of Bridge Street, about four doors north of Cayuga street. Note the gasoline pump in front of the store.

The new store, named H. L. Richards and Company, featured electric lights, a tin ceiling, open shelving, a well-stocked cigar counter, and a candy counter. Horace worked until 1918, when his son Earl took over. Earl stands near the scale at the far right of the photograph.

The photograph above shows Bridge Street looking north. On the right side is the Waldmere hotel, then Harper's Lunchroom. On the left is Brian Lee's Meat Market, where the meetings of the early county officers were held. The large brick building was the Nixon-Densmore building, and just beyond that was Banowske's tailor shop. Shown below is a postcard looking south on Bridge Street around the same time period. On the right is A. R. Wooton's Drugstore. One door south was the barbershop, with a street sign advertising "Baths." Next was Flye Hardware with a gasoline pump out front. In the intersection of Bridge and Broad Streets is the "silent policeman," a traffic sign advising cars to "Keep To The Right." The advent of cars made the sign necessary. On the left was White's Bazaar, Kearney Township Hall, and the Bellaire Bank across Broad Street.

The Kearney Township Hall was built in 1883 and later razed in 1934. The land, at the northeast corner of Bridge and Broad Streets, was purchased for $100 from James M. Wadsworth and his wife, Ruth, of Central Lake and Elisa Cook of Bellaire on May 10, 1882. Township offices as well as the county offices were on the first floor until the county courthouse was completed in 1905, and the county offices moved. On the second floor was the opera house, and it was here that many community events were held: school graduations, school plays, and many fund-raising events. The opera house had floor space for dances as well as a stage. Traveling shows, such as *Uncle Tom's Cabin*, were performed here. The special entrance was at the rear of the building, and eventually a ramp was built to facilitate the moving of the trunks and stage scenery used by the traveling shows.

KEARNEY TOWNHALL
GONE!
BUILT IN 1884

This photograph shows Kearney Township Hall after 1900 with many changes: A covered entrance to the opera house was added at the rear of the building on Broad Street, and the fire bell was removed. The two gentlemen in the street are identified as John Montgomery (right) and attorney Roswell Leavitt. The buildings to the north on Bridge Street are Aunt Jane's Bazaar and the Waldmere Hotel. Aunt Jane's building was originally the location of Bellaire's first newspaper, the *Bellaire Breeze*, run by Albert S. Abbott from 1881 through 1896. The building behind the hall on Broad Street was the county jail and sheriff's residence. After the county offices moved into the new courthouse in 1905, Kearney Township began to renovate the building. A larger stage with a new curtain was constructed in the opera house, and a room was planned for the combined Kearney and Forest Home Townships' libraries.

The second hotel in Bellaire, the Inter Lake, was located on the east side of Bridge Street, north of the Kearney Township Hall. It was built in 1881 for Roswell Leavitt, the attorney who defended the right of the supervisors to move the county seat from Elk Rapids to Bellaire in the Supreme Court. A widower with two very young sons, Clyde and Scott, Leavitt made the hotel his home and his office. In 1894, the hotel was expanded, and the name changed to Waldmere. Others managed the hotel at various times through the years. In 1884, the hotel letterhead read, "Temperance House, Oscar W. Kibby, Proprietor. Good barn and livery. Special attention to commercial men and tourists. Boats furnished at reasonable rates." Proprietors leased the building and furnished all the necessary equipment, including furniture, to run the hotel. Mr. and Mrs. W. J. Osborne were caretakers during the time that the hotel was updated with a new foundation and a cement walkway to replace the boardwalk.

The village of Bellaire is contained within two townships, Forest Home and Kearney, divided by the Intermediate River. John Collins ran the Forest Home House on the west side of Bridge Street north of the river. A family member wrote the following description on the back of this c. 1900 photograph: "This is the picture of the 'barn,' as Dad called it." Arrows indicated John Collins along with his wife, Sarah, and daughter Bertha. Joining them for a ride were John and Laura Reefer and children.

In spring 1908, John H. Collins leased a building from Henry Richardi and opened the Riverside Hotel. An interior photograph taken in January 1911 shows the front entry of the hotel featuring a well-stocked cigar counter with clerk John Ritt ready to be of service. Seated in the area are John Collins and his son Basil. The 1910 census lists Aleda Peck, Lena Ellis, and Gladys DeLosh as servants.

The Collins family portrait shows John Collins, wife Sarah, daughters Bertha (white bow) and Bertine, son Basil, and an unidentified infant.

John H. Collins's Riverside Hotel was located on the west side of Bridge Street, near the south bank of the Intermediate River.

The Riverside Hotel was destroyed by the July 1921 fire, which began in a barn just north of the hotel. This fire destroyed 11 buildings in the village, and because of high winds, even buildings blocks away were destroyed. Word went out to neighboring fire departments as far away as Traverse City. The first to arrive was the East Jordan group, who came by train. The fire was stopped by the Nixon Store, which was brick, and an unexpected rainstorm.

Bellaire, Mich.

The Bellaire Bank, on the southeast corner of Bridge and Broad Streets, was the first cement-block structure in the village. Built by Osbert Dandelion Tiffany of the banking family, it was constructed in 1904. Local builder Charles S. Wilcox drew up the plans for the building—a two-story, double-front building with a stairway in between. Tiffany purchased Coltrin molds in Grand Rapids, and the blocks were made in the gravel pit west of the Bellaire schoolhouse. The local paper published a complete description of this unique new building material. The post office was located in the back portion of the building. Next door, the building was occupied by Hugh Coldren's Furniture and Funeral, and the family lived on the upper floor. In August 1906, Frederick W. Bechtold, of the woodenware company, purchased the banking interest of Sickles and Tiffany Company and with a substantial investment created the Bellaire State Bank. The new officers were F. W. Bechtold, president; Dr. William A. Evans, vice president; and Osbert Tiffany, cashier.

The current community hall—built over a period of years through government programs including the CWA, ERA, and WPA—was built where Kearney Township Hall once stood. Dedicated on July 9, 1937, the township sold an interest in the building to the Village of Bellaire. The facilities provided a stage, dressing rooms, basketball court, and balcony on upstairs level, and in the basement was a full kitchen, banquet hall, shower facilities for school athletes, public library, and public toilets. Jane White, who owned the building next door, made the size of the building possible through a land donation.

In this photograph of an early log run in the spring around 1900, the background on the left shows a corner of the woodenware factory, and also on the left is the first gristmill in the village. On the right is the Richardi and Bechtold Sawmill, with a large audience in the foreground watching the run. The young boy at right appears to be handling the logs in fine style.

This photograph, taken around 1903, features the Richardi and Bechtold Sawmill on the east side of Bridge Street and the house that served as the company headquarters. What appears to be a road is actually an elevated walkway, which led to the "Terrace," or the hillside across the river. This walkway shortened the path into the village for the hillside residents. At one point, the village decided to forgo the repairs needed for the walkway, and residents on the hillside withheld their taxes until the repairs were done. The house, which was the headquarters for the factory, survived three fires, eventually succumbing to the 1921 fire.

Robert Richardi and Fredrick Bechtold met in St. Louis, Missouri, and formed a partnership to take advantage of the forests of Northern Michigan, founding the Richardi and Bechtold Woodenware Company. They built their first sawmill in 1879, and it was destroyed by fire in 1897. Robert Richardi had been in the woodenware industry and held patents on some designs. In 1898, the company was reformed, and woodenware became the primary product, shipping as far as Australia, New Zealand, and South Africa. Their San Francisco agent (who wrote a complete description of the earthquake there) apologized for being out of business.

The Richardi and Bechtold Woodenware Company factory burned to the ground in 1905. This photograph shows the factory where about 65 men were employed, with a clothespin department employing 12 women. This was the only department in which females could work. It was in this building that all the woodenware was produced. At one time, the clothespin department was so far behind in their orders that they needed four railroad cars for shipping. The ladies were led from the fire by their supervisor down a sliding ramp from their place on the second floor, but they lost all their personal goods. The financial loss of this one building was placed at $50,000 with little insurance coverage.

The Richardi and Bechtold Sawmill was the second building lost in the 1905 fire. As one of the village's largest employers, it was a large community loss. The fire broke out on a Friday afternoon and soon engulfed the entire area. The large piles of cut lumber and bolts ready for the woodenware factory supplied a constant source of fuel. Firefighters were largely trying to save adjoining property. The planning mill of Cook and Wilcox was saved by a citizen bucket brigade, and the same was true for the J. E. Richards lumberyard. As the newspaper reported, "Bucket Lines Do Excellent Service."

RICHARDI & BECHTOLD,

Chopping Trays
Vinegar Measures
Patent Scoops
Clothes Pins
Maple Bowls

MANUFACTURERS OF

Woodenware Specialties, Kitchen, Dairy, Bakery and Confectionery Utensils.

Butter Moulds
Rolling Pins
Butter Ladles
Potato Mashe
Etc.

BELLAIRE, MICH.,   Nov. 4, 'O

TO OUR FRIENDS:

We regret that we are again obliged to advise you that we have had the misfortune to lose one of our factories by fire but are pleased to state that, with a few exceptions, we are able to take care of your orders for the present.

We take this opportunity to express our thanks for your past favors and assure you that we will appreciate any favors you may turn our way.

Yours very truly,

RICHARDI & BECHTOLD,

Per

Manager.

The 1905 fire was a disaster for the Richardi and Bechtold Woodenware Company. Having rebuilt after two previous fires, the decision was made not to rebuild. The area had very little standing timber left and certainly not enough to justify the expense of rebuilding both the sawmill and woodenware factory. The above letter was sent to their clients; however, William G. Warren's mill in Bellaire could make enough product to fill the outstanding orders. A collection of shipping orders for July 1907 confirms that, under the corporate name, orders were going out to as many as 52 stores, many of which were Woolworth stores.

The Charlevoix Light Plant was built on land that was formerly the site of the Richardi and Bechtold Sawmill. Henry Richardi contracted with the City of Charlevoix to furnish them with electricity. The work began in 1905, and in September 1906, the generators started up and electric current flowed into the Charlevoix lighting system. As part of this arrangement, Robert Douglas secured the contract from Hydraulic Light and Power Company to procure and distribute the 1,000 poles needed to string the wires from Bellaire to Charlevoix. Most of the poles had to be at least 30 feet in height. Douglas was to place the poles in a line for others to set, a line that was 25 miles long. In the background of this photograph is the Richardi House.

Bathing Beach Bellaire, Mich.

Richardi Park, just north of the Intermediate River on the east side of Bridge Street, is located on the land originally occupied by the Richardi and Bechtold Woodenware Company factory and sawmill. Around 1925, Henry Richardi, before moving to California, deeded the land to the village for a park. Through the years, the park area had been used as a rubbish dump, including the material from the Kearney Township Hall. In September 1934, county agricultural agent Kenneth Ousterhaut landscaped the area, with Grant Mudge as the engineer. Ed Foster was the foreman in charge of the ERA project that employed about 25 men. They graded the land, planted trees and shrubs, fixed the shoreline, and built a rustic shelter to hold picnic tables and benches. The camp stove was added outside the shelter. The park and beach was a boon to the local families.

Five

HISTORIC HOMES

Around 1900, a photographer set up his equipment on the steep hillside area now referred to as the Terrace to take this picture of the village. He was looking east, and the picture captures everything north of the Bridge Street Bridge. Many of the houses pictured still stand and are maintained as private residences. The population of Bellaire in 1906 was 1,170, a large increase from the 1882 census, which was 233 people. This spike in population was largely due to the woodenware factory, the white 12-window building shown at the water's edge. Employment at one time was as high as 145 men in the factory and 12 women in the clothespin department. Other buildings visible are the Methodist church with its stately steeple, directly across the street from the Richardi House, and the Tiffany House with its noticeable turret, located at the north edge of town.

The Grand Victorian (the Richardi House) is one of only two buildings in Antrim County listed on the National Register of Historic Places. Today it is a charming bed and breakfast inn. Pictured on books, magazines, and cereal and cracker boxes, this famous Richardi House was built by Henry Richardi in 1895. A master of woodenware and the sciences, Richardi put the latest design and technology into the home. It not only boasts incredible Queen Anne Victorian architecture but was also the first home in the area with electricity, central heat, and indoor plumbing.

Dr. Carlton Hinman, a local homeopathic physician, built this late Victorian-style home in 1905. The house has the distinction of being the only yellow brick house on Bridge Street and being the first brick house in Bellaire. The brick came from the brickyard located on South M-88, which was leased by Dr. Hinman and his father-in-law, Erwin Hemstreet. From the stair-landing window, an interesting view can be seen of the Methodist church steeple and the village.

The Erwin Hemstreet house on the corner of Bridge and First Streets is one of two identical homes built by Hemstreet. The houses were renovated in 1896, and because of their architectural style, they were referred to as cottages. Later several other homes built with windows in their rooflines were given the cottage-style label. Hemstreet was in several business ventures, often with his son-in-law, Dr. Hinman.

Standing quite far back from Park Street is the Nixon house, now known as the Bellaire Bed and Breakfast. William J. Nixon and his wife, Emma (Richardi), built the house in 1878. The Nixons had a successful grocery store business. Emma is a sister to Henry Richardi. The house has been restored to much of its early condition, plus a small dollhouse (an outer construction) built for the Nixon daughters still stands.

In 1904, Osbert Dandelion Tiffany purchased this house at a cost of $2,700. According to architectural tradition, most small towns had at least one "castle" built during the Victorian period. Bellaire has more than one, and the Tiffany House, with its several turrets, certainly qualifies. Tiffany and his wife, Mila, lived in the house until 1907. He was treasurer of the woodenware factory and partner in the local bank.

On September 15, 1901, the *Bellaire Independent* headlined the article "Dr. Arthur Bodle's house is nearly ready for occupancy." The house, located on River Street (presently Cayuga Street) with a small tower in the northeast corner and beautiful art-glass windows throughout, is listed as having Gothic-style architecture. In 1916, Dr. Bodle, while in route to a Forest Home Township home for a medical call, died of a heart attack. The house stands empty today.

Clark and Harriet Densmore moved into their new home on Cayuga Street in November 1895 with four children, and there they raised three more. Upon their death, two daughters spent their summers in the home. In 1973, their granddaughter Margie and her husband, John Fleet, moved into the home and raised their five children there. Today their grandchildren are the fifth generation to enjoy the home with many visits and family gatherings.

In 1905, W. A. Hosmer, according to the *Bellaire Independent*, built this home for $4,000. It was also reported that "the red pressed brick is the same as used for the new Antrim County Court House." Hosmer, a successful businessman, owned a sawmill in Bellaire. Today a senior citizen park that bears the name Hosmer Park is located on the street behind the house. The property for the park was donated by the Hosmer family.

On December 10, 1879, at a meeting of the Antrim County Board of Supervisors, plans were approved for a new sheriff residence and jail to be built at the new county seat of Bellaire. The jail was completed in 1881 with an addition in 1895. The sheriff lived in the front, and the jail was the building situated behind the house. It is now a law office for Jack Unger.

Six

THEY PROUDLY SERVED

This photograph shows the Grand Army of the Republic in Bellaire after 1908 in front of the old Nixon building 43 years after the Civil War (1860–1865). Civil War veterans, from left to right, are (first row) unidentified, Emanuel Dunson, Zachary Johnson, John Bush, and William May; (second row) Haney Alcott, unidentified, John Willis, Solomon Dewey, George Montgomery, and Stephen Eldred; (third row) Reuben Martin, Henry Stewart, Jacob Watrous, Roswell Leavitt, George Humeston (flag), unidentified, George Cabanis, Frederick Bechtold, and Edward Carpenter.

This memorial stone, at the corner of Bridge and Broad Streets, was given by the Blue Star Mothers and Wives Club of Bellaire commemorating soldiers of World War II. Engraved on the plaque are the benevolent words befitting all wars: "In honor of the men and women who served in World War II and in memory of those who made the supreme sacrifice."

This picture shows an unidentified Civil War drummer.

Harley Bump Smith (1879–1949) attended Eddy School in Kearney Township. He entered the Spanish-American War at the age of 19 and was assigned to the 35th Michigan Volunteers Company B. The Smith family can make claim that in every war beginning with the Civil War a family member has proudly served his country. Smith is buried at the Bellaire Lakeview Cemetery in the below photograph. (Courtesy of daughter Aethale Smith Chapman.)

HARLEY BUMP SMITH
US ARMY
SPANISH AMERICAN WAR
1879   1949

Scott Leavitt

J. Barwise, Class 1898

Bellaire, Mich.

Scott Leavitt (1879–1966) graduated from Bellaire High School in 1898. He went on to represent the State of Montana in Washington, D.C., in the U.S. House of Representatives. Scott also held the office of national commander of the Spanish-American War veterans. He was the brother of Clyde Leavitt and son of Roswell Leavitt, the first prosecuting attorney for Antrim County. Bellaire volunteers of the 35th Michigan Volunteers in the Spanish-American War of 1898 included Pvt. Frank C. Bedell, Company B; Pvt. William E. Cooper, Company B; Pvt. John Fischer, Company C; Pvt. Clyde Leavitt, Company B; Cpl. Scott Leavitt, Company L; Pvt. Herbert Macus, Company B; Pvt. John A. McPherson, Company B; Pvt. Henry A. Newberry, Company B; Pvt. Harry W. Price, Company B; Pvt. Cornelius J. Roach, Company D; Pvt. Harley B. Smith, Company B; and Pvt. Walter Wright, Company B.

Cpl. Frank Marshall May attended Bellaire High School. While a member of the Michigan National Guard, Marshall's unit was called up to go to Texas to help secure the U.S. border due to threatening activity of Pancho Villa. While still in Texas, World War I was declared and his unit, the "Fighting Fifth," was sent to the war front in France. (Courtesy of nephew Craig Smith.)

In March 1917, Antrim County World War I soldiers left for service. Among them were Ola Dewey (Canadian uniform), Earl Richards, Coryell Sevrey, Fred Moran, Leo Thomas, Clyde Griffin, Clarence Smith, Earl Kinnison, Henry Strehl, Edward Wiltse, Gordon Kirby, James Loper, Newel Cross, ? Butler, Clarence Johnson, ? Donaldson, William VandeVenter, ? Krantz, Robert Alspaugh, Bun Anderson, Charles Erwin, and Edward Hartman. Sheriff Andrew Dunsmore (sixth row) sees the soldiers off.

Pictured here in 1922 is the Woman's Relief Corps, Auxiliary to the Grand Amy of the Republic. Their mission was to care for the veteran and his dependent ones and perpetuate the memory of their heroic dead. The corps was nationally established in 1883; the Bellaire Weber Post No. 206 was established between 1888 and 1933. Pictured from left to right are (first row) Eliza Thomas, two unidentified, Mary Humeston, and Clarissa Underhill; (second row) two unidentified, Dora Kibby, Ida Childs, Dessie Dickerson, Ena Fuller, two unidentified, Lola (Hemstreet) Hinman, and ? Waite.

Maybelle (Lessard) Thomas (1894–1992) was eligible to join the auxiliary through her husband, World War I veteran Herbert Thomas. Just as the Woman's Relief Corps was disbanding, Maybelle, serving as first president, and 24 other charter members founded the American Legion Auxiliary Post No. 247 (1933–1977). As post historian, she was ardent in her belief that the history of local veterans should be collected and preserved, as confirmed by the many Thomas scrapbooks at the museum.

Seven

LAKE BELLAIRE RESORT COUNTRY

Map
of
BELLAIRE RESORT COUNTRY

How to Reach

Bellaire is located on State Trunk Line M-88 midway between U.S.-31 and U.S.-131. For the season of 1929 U.S.-31 is routed directly through Bellaire. To reach Bellaire by way of U.S.-131 follow this trunk line to Mancelona and from there take M-88.

Through Pullman trains daily from Detroit and Chicago, making through connections with southern cities.

LEGEND
Trunk Line
County Roads
Railroads

SCALE OF MILES

Bellaire Area Historical Society

After lumbering ceased to be profitable, farming and resorts became the next source of income. On Grass Lake, just south of Bellaire, resorts began to appear. Among them were Fisherman's Paradise, Miley's Lodge, Lake View, and North Lakes Resort. What started out as fishing trips for the men soon evolved into family vacations. Over the years, camping progressed from tents to cabins then to commercial lodges. Many of these early vacationers bought lakefront property and built their own summer homes on the shores of Grass Lake. The lake name was changed to Lake Bellaire around 1930.

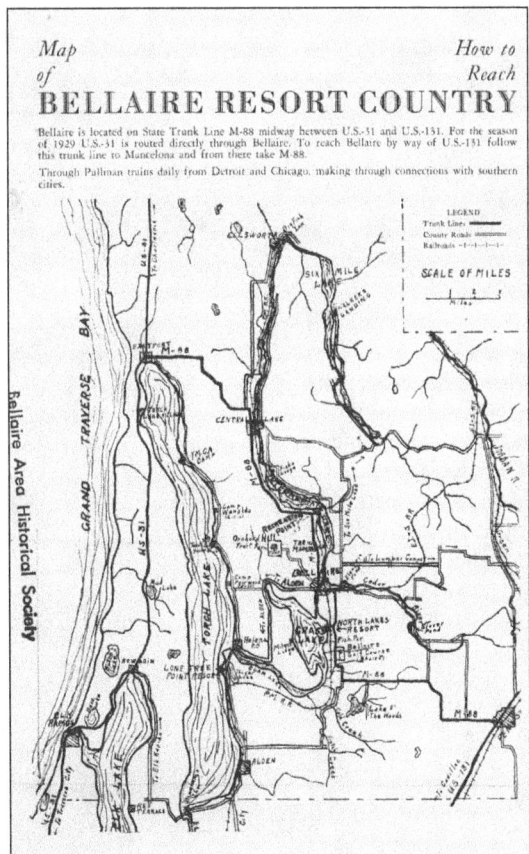

99

Horace Delano Smith, a Bellaire resident, was self-employed as a sign painter, furniture refinisher, house painter, wallpaper hanger, dance teacher, penmanship teacher, and fishing guide. He was known as "H.D.," never Horace. Few issues of the *Bellaire Independent* did not carry an article noting his local work. He painted outdoor signs for merchants and decorated the interiors of large homes and business establishments. He was mentioned in the paper simply as "the painter." His advertisements stated, "I have the best line of sample wallpaper ever shown in the region, at prices beyond competition. Satisfaction guaranteed." Smith married Henrietta Rockfellow in 1884. His two daughters from this marriage were Lera (1887–1965) and Una (1889–1924).

One of Smith's talents was penmanship, which he taught in Bellaire in 1898. He advertised in the local newspapers offering a private class. He drew a very fancy advertisement for this class. He did school graduation diplomas for a Petoskey school. This reproduction is his own signature. As the *Bellaire Independent* reported, he had thus signed the Bellaire House hotel register, but no one could read who had signed in.

Smith's first Fisherman's Paradise was a cabin located at Crystal Springs, adjacent to Clam Lake. It was leased from Elvira Brownson in 1905. The lease was renewed for the years 1906–1908. The family ran the camp while Smith served as a fishing guide for the men who contracted for his services. In the years 1909 and 1910, Smith leased land from Ernest Biladeau on the east side of Grass Lake. The land was purchased by Dale Miley in January 1910, and the two men formed a partnership. In the spring, the partners raised a large lodge, and the Smith family moved in for the summer. In October 1910, the lodge burned to the ground. This was a total loss for both men, and the partnership was dissolved. The family had lost all its possessions. The canoe named *Unalera* was Smith's way of honoring his two daughters, Una and Lera.

Starting over with investors and a new location, Smith started his third Fisherman's Paradise on the southeast side of Grass Lake. Beginning with tents on platforms for the guests and a communal dining room, the resort opened on May 25, 1911. Guests came from Cleveland and Detroit. Using his distinctive penmanship, Smith designed a letterhead for his weekly column in the *Bellaire Independent*. All new arrivals were noted as well as entertainers. The largest catches of fish were entered in the news. The guests often provided special entertainment and shared their catch of the day.

Smith found that many guests at his resort were interested in Native American lore, so he hired a Native American woman to demonstrate her skills at basket weaving and a father and son from Elk Rapids to create a dugout. Working with axes on site, father John Pawabska (below) and son Peter Pawabska (right) made a dugout that measured 5.5 yards in length and 26 inches wide at its center. These pictures were taken in 1927. Smith carried the Native American theme into his own persona, wearing buckskin outfits and, at times, a feathered bonnet. He called himself "the Indian" and had a launch named *The Indian*.

The "Indian" Teaching Archery
Fisherman's Paradise, Bell[...], Mich

Peter and John Pawabska pose next to their handcrafted dugout above. At left, Smith is pictured in full Native American regalia teaching a guest the art of using a bow and arrow. He was a great promoter and missed very few opportunities to capitalize on events. Gene Stratton Porter's "Limberlost" stories were at the height of popularity, which resulted in the following write-up in the 1904 *Fisherman's News*: "The Indian accompanied a bunch of women through the 'Limberlost' Wednesday. All pronounced it the most remarkable piece of virgin forest they had ever visited. Of course, when fences came in the line of travel, some boosting had to be done, and the guide had to turn his eyes away on many occasions."

By the fall of 1916, Smith was ready to collect materials for his new lodge. He purchased additional lakefront property and advertised for 150 loads of stone and gravel at $100 a load. Construction began in September, and in July 1917, *Fisherman's News* announced, "Sunday dinner was served for the first time in the new building." For the grand opening, local talent was hired: Chester Maltby (a great tenor), Lyle Dickerson, Thelma Frank, Maybelle Corey, Edgar Bacon, and others. The kitchen was run by Smith's daughter Lera, who was trained as a chef at the Blackstone Hotel in Chicago.

Smith's lodge was artistically planned with roomy, light and airy spaces and a fine outlook toward the lake. The dining room could seat 200 guests and soon became a favorite spot for the Bellaire merchants and families to have Sunday dinner. Each guest was recorded in the hotel register—even those who just came for dinner. The lodge also welcomed large groups, such as the Kalbaska Board of Trade, many junior-senior high school banquets, and on May 22, 1022, the Bellaire alumni banquet. The mammoth fireplace was built by local craftsman Morris Wellman.

Ballaire Golf Course, Bellaire, Mich.

In January 1925, Smith, while in Detroit, began collecting information on golf courses with the intent of creating one in connection with Fisherman's Paradise. Smith retained the services of Duncan Rose, one of the best golf-grounds experts in the country, to lay out the new course. The course opened in 1927 on M-88, three miles south of Bellaire. Pictured is an unidentified group on the first tee. This was at a time when gentlemen wore "plus-fours," had small golf bags, hired caddies, and walked the course. The fourth fairway featured a water hazard, complete with trout.

Golf Course, Bellaire, Mich.

After the disastrous 1910 fire, Dale J. Miley, owner and proprietor of Miley's Resort on the west side of Grass Lake, built a new lodge in 1911. He also had several small cottages built at the lakeshore. The original farmhouse became the dining facility and a home for Miley's mother. During the 1930s, Miley advertised special events to celebrate the Fourth of July at the resort. He would have guests picked up at the marina and taken to the festivities by boat. (Below, courtesy of "Bud" Cowles.)

Lake View Resort
On Grass Lake, Bellaire, Mich.

In the spring of 1911, Anson T. Schoolcraft purchased some of the original cottages on the east side of Grass Lake and opened the Lake View Resort. His 1923 brochure listed the following attractions: "An ideal place, safe for children, bathing, and playing in the woods." It offered excellent fishing and "a dining room supplied with fresh vegetables, chicken and eggs from our own farm." Rates were $3 per day and $15 to $21 per week. The resort was open from June 15 to September 15. Plus, patrons would be picked up in Bellaire at no charge. The resort also offered first-class rowboats free of charge to the guests.

In 1910, brothers Chester "Chet" and William "Bill" Maltby purchased two old cottages on the east side of Grass Lake, one being the Charles Wiffenbach summer home. There they established the North Lakes Resort. For Chet, a schoolteacher, this was a summer project. After two years, Bill gave up his interest, and Chet continued the resort for 49 years. He expanded the resort by purchasing the adjacent Lake View Resort. Beginning in simpler times, there was no cocktail hour, no dressing for dinner, and no planned activities. Chet operated an old-style family resort. (Below, courtesy of Laura Sexton.)

Eight

THIS AND THAT

The following is an excerpt from the *Bellaire Independent* on August 6, 1908: "About a dozen members of the 'Buckeye Fishing Club' of Columbus, Ohio, arrived in Bellaire Wednesday morning, to prepare a place on the west shore of Grass lake for the remainder of the club members who will arrive in a few days."

by 1.B TROUT
CAUGHT AT
BELLAIRE BY E.DICKINSON
AUG 1913

L-1311

Fishing was an attraction for many people from Ohio, and for the locals, nothing was as highly celebrated as the opening of trout season in May. The local press devoted considerable space to reporting the success of local anglers. May often found the local residents trying their luck at the river's edge in town. In 1906, Mrs. Flanagan caught 30 trout. On May 5, 1910, A. B. Wooton and his wife caught 23 nice ones, William Hierlihy caught 24, and George Maltby caught 39. Pictured at left is E. Dickerson with his nice catch in 1913. The other angler and his child (below) are not identified, but he surely had a nice catch.

An 1898 newspaper reported, "Deep Water Landing was finished and it can be reached by following a southerly extension of Bridge Street for a half mile or so until it intersects the Intermediate River." Smaller steamers, such as the *Mabel*, used the marina at Warner Bridge on River (Cayuga) Street. Both locations were used for excursion trips down the "Chain of Lakes" to Elk Rapids until 1917. In later years, cottage owners boated to the marina and delivered their grocery list to the store. Upon returning to their boat, they found the groceries carefully packed for the trip home.

The boathouses on the Intermediate River near Deep Water Point were built to house the launches of the local merchants; many owned cottages on the east shore of Grass Lake.

Many launches were built by local citizens, in particular "Skipper" Bedell and Elmer E. Dickinson. The gasoline meters were purchased from John D. Adams, agent for the "Eclipse" motors built in neighboring Mancelona. The local paper noted that "Oscar W. Kibby has deserted old style oar-locomotion and purchased an 'Eclipse' engine."

Dredging the Intermediate River was essential to the economic life of the village. An annual spring event was the cleaning of the river so logs could enter Grass Lake and beyond. The L. G. Smith Company of Grand Rapids was hired to do the job for which the village paid. The river was used by one and all to get rid of their trash, and with several mills on its borders, it did slow the flow of water.

What a difference a few years make: Instead of a log run, the river at Bridge Street in 1909 was the scene of a Fourth of July game. A tug-of-war between Forest Home Township and Kearney Township occurred here. Forest Home won the event. In the background is the Charlevoix Light Plant and the Richardi and Bechtold Woodenware Company office building.

Early settlers were required by law to make and maintain the roads in their districts. This photograph shows one such crew, unidentified, at work. Overseers were voted into office. Under State Act No. 243 of 1881, landowners were accessed for taxes and for the number of days they had to work on the roads.

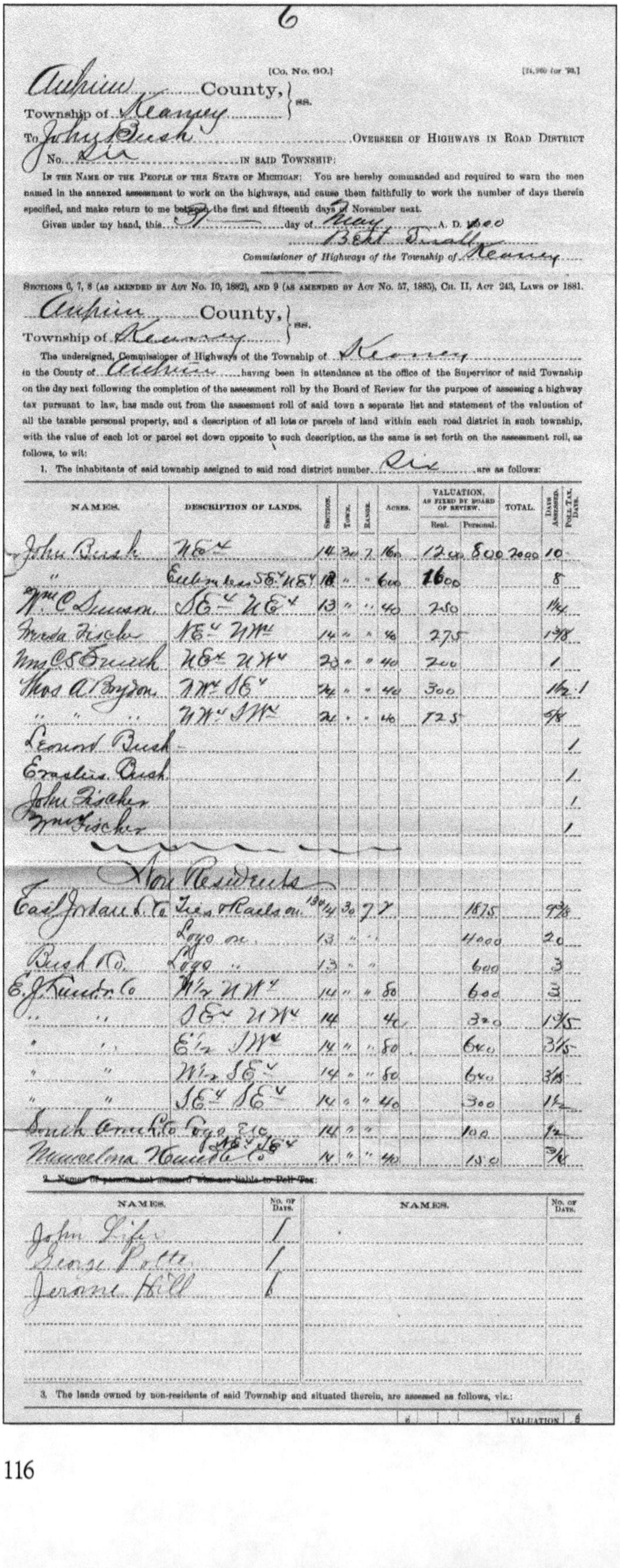

6

[Co. No. 60.] [14,900 for '93.]

Antrim County, } ss.
Township of Kearney }

To John Bush, Overseer of Highways in Road District No. Six in said Township:

In the Name of the People of the State of Michigan: You are hereby commanded and required to warn the men named in the annexed assessment to work on the highways, and cause them faithfully to work the number of days therein specified, and make return to me between the first and fifteenth days of November next.

Given under my hand, this 9 day of May A. D. 1900

Bert Tisdall

Commissioner of Highways of the Township of Kearney

Sections 6, 7, 8 (as amended by Act No. 10, 1882), and 9 (as amended by Act No. 57, 1885), Ch. II, Act 243, Laws of 1881.

Antrim County, } ss.
Township of Kearney }

The undersigned, Commissioner of Highways of the Township of Kearney in the County of Antrim having been in attendance at the office of the Supervisor of said Township on the day next following the completion of the assessment roll by the Board of Review for the purpose of assessing a highway tax pursuant to law, has made out from the assessment roll of said town a separate list and statement of the valuation of all the taxable personal property, and a description of all lots or parcels of land within each road district in such township, with the value of each lot or parcel set down opposite to such description, as the same is set forth on the assessment roll, as follows, to wit:

1. The inhabitants of said township assigned to said road district number Six are as follows:

Names.	Description of Lands.	Section.	Town.	Range.	Acres.	Valuation, as fixed by Board of Review. Real.	Personal.	Total.	Days Assessed.	Poll Tax Days.
John Bush	NE¼	14	30	7	160	1200	800	2000	10	
"	Eubanks SE¼ NE¼	18	"	"	600	1600			8	
Wm C Duncan	SE¼ NE¼	13	"	"	40	250			1¼	
Frieda Fischer	NE¼ NW¼	14	"	"	40	275			1⅜	
Mrs C S Bunch	NE¼ NW¼	23	"	"	40	200			1	
Thos A Boydon	NW¼ SE¼	14	"	"	40	300			1½	1
" "	NW¼ SW¼	24	"	"	40	125			⅝	
Leonard Bush										1
Erastus Bush										1
John Fischer										1
Wm Fischer										1
Non Residents										
East Jordan L. Co	Ties & Rails on	13 & 14	30	7	7		1875		9⅜	
	Logs on	13	"	"			4000		20	
Bush Co.	Logs "	13	"	"			600		3	
E. J. Kunde Co	W½ NW¼	14	"	"	80		600		3	
" "	SE¼ NW¼	14			40		320		1⅗	
" "	E½ SW¼	14	"	"	80		640		3⅕	
" "	W½ SE¼	14	"	"	80		640		3⅕	
" "	SE¼ SE¼	14	"	"	40		300		1½	
~~South Arm L. Co~~	Logs Etc	14	"	"			100		½	
Mancelona Handle Co	NE¼ SE¼	14	"	"	40		150		¾	

~~2. Names of persons not assessed who are liable to Poll Tax:~~

Names.	No. of Days.	Names.	No. of Days.
John Sifer	1		
George Potter	1		
Jerome Hill	1		

3. The lands owned by non-residents of said Township and situated therein, are assessed as follows, viz.:

			Valuation	

This form was used by the elected road commissioners for each township to report the assessment of taxes and hours of labor that each "Free holders" whose property adjoined the road was to pay. This was reported to the state.

Important to the life of the village was the livery stable, run by various owners in the past years. Among them was Andrew Dole, who also had a livery in Mancelona. He also operated the stagecoach line between the two villages before it was disbanded in 1910. The Bellaire livery was located on Broad Street across from the courthouse. The business was purchased by Edward H. Maltby around 1900. His three sons, "Pete" (Harold), "Bill" (William), and "Chet" (Chester), grew up in the business. The Livery and Dray was a good business until the automobile took over. In preparing for the future, Maltby became an agent for Standard Oil in 1927. His son Pete continued as the agent after his father retired. Pictured below is Antrim County's first snowmobile, built by Pete around 1923.

In 1905, president Donna Petrie opened the first meeting of the Ladies Literary Club. The 20 women of the club stated that their purpose was community and personal improvement. To fulfill this purpose, one lady was chosen as a critic. Her position was to find and correct any errors in grammar, language, program presentation, and in the discussion that followed. The first club dues of $1 each were to be used for materials for the activities for the club. Later, as times changed, the dues were raised. Scholarships were given to special female graduates of the high school, and gifts were given to the Bellaire library and museums for their improvement. Today the Ladies Literary Club still fulfills its purpose. The times and participants may have changed, but the ideal of personal and community improvement has never been allowed to fade. This studio portrait of the literary club is not dated but could be of the original 20 members. From left to right are (first row) Elizabeth Gray, Nellie Deevy, and Miss Young; (second row) Stacie Kaufman, Mrs. Allen, Mrs. Frank, Mrs. Large, Mrs. Young, and Kitty Coldren; (third row) Mary Craven, Mrs. Grawn, Lottie Corey, Maximiliana Bechtold, Jennie Gordon, Luella Kirkland, and Mary Bansil; (fourth row) Minnie Montague, Louise Robinson, Lizzie Nichols, and Donna Petrie.

Photographed in 1904, local members of the Women's Christian Temperance Union are, from left to right, (first row) Ida Childs, Elizabeth Eldred, Lenora Wilcox, Mrs. Harrison, Mrs. Hill, Lena Guiles, Sarah Cleveland, and Harriet Ballhouse; (second row) Thila Dickerson (behind Childs), Mrs. Reiley, Carrie Thomas, Shely May, Emma Nixon, and Margaret May; (third row) Lizzie Nippress and Mary Adamson; (fourth row) Mrs. Phelps, Mrs. Ball, Mrs. W. Robinson and son, Mrs. A. C. Tiffany, Mila Tiffany, and Margaret Potter. (First names, if known, were added by researchers.) The union often sponsored parades, such as the one pictured below marching south on Bridge Street. The ladies were rewarded for their efforts in 1910 when Antrim County became dry, with the exception of Jordan Township.

Founded around October 1906, some of the members of the Bellaire chapter of the Fraternal Benefit Society of Modern Woodmen of America are Richard Clapp, Derwood Pendock, Judea Cross, Edwin J. Potter, Peter and George Fate, and George Sanford. The group, known as foresters, raised money for charity and sold low-cost insurance for families. The receipt shown below is for $12 paid to Samuel Adams for the rental of a hall on December 26, 1901.

Nearly every village had a cornet band, and Bellaire was no exception. In 1902, the director was Edward James Gray, a local photographer. The band played at many community events. Members on the above postcard are, from left to right, (first row) Leroy Gray (the director's son); (second row) John Ticknor, Leon Cook, Charles May, and Mr. Martin; (third row) Arthur Ward, Hayward Noteware, Edward Gray (bandleader), Herman Dickerson, and Manuel "Manny" Kaufman. Elizabeth Gray was a music teacher, and the family, on several occasions, entertained guests at the Fisherman's Paradise resort. A later photograph, taken on the front porch of the Riverside Hotel, shows a much larger band with the Collins family—from left to right, Sarah, Bertine, Basil, and John—in the background. The band members were not identified.

The original Bellaire Stars baseball team listed in this *c.* 1901 studio photograph are 1.) Lloyd Woodruff, 2.) Cyrus Glass, 3.) George Wilson, 4.) Charles Brownson, 5.) Fred Alcott, 6.) Frank Dunn, 7.) Hayward Noteware, 8.) John Stanley, 9.) Bert A. Dole, 10.) Charles Partlow, 11.) Osro "Chub" MacIntire, 12.) Hugh Coldren (manager), and 13.) Ira Adams (president). The club was reorganized in 1902 and 1903, and it won most of its games against professional and semiprofessional teams. The Stars beat one team decisively that had not lost a game in three years. Baseball was the predominate sport, and rivalry between villages was intense. The teams had paid pitchers and catchers, but the rest of the team was volunteers. On occasion an entire game, inning by inning, was printed on the front page of the paper. In later photographs, around 1913 and 1914, Ira Adams was still president, but the manager was Bill Sampson, a local barber.

This photograph was taken in 1917 at the dedication of a 100-foot flagpole on the courthouse lawn. In 1875, the Bellaire village plat shows the courthouse square, and in 1879, the county supervisors hired George McKay to clear the square. He was paid $225 to chop, grub, and clear all stumps, then plow and grade. Until 1904, the land was used as the baseball diamond. The courthouse was completed in 1905, without clocks in the tower. Local firefighters began a clock fund, and many people donated. Even the Fairwood Boys' Camp put on a stage show and donated the proceeds. In 1923, the *Bellaire Independent* listed the major donors: Charles S. Smith: $26.50; H. D. Smith: $26; Judge C. L. Bailey: $25; and W. S. Mesick: $25. The clock was installed in that year.

Mamie and Marion Mull, niece and nephew of Earl Henderson, sit in the oxcart in front of the Bellaire House hotel on Bridge Street. Gwendolyn Large sits in the car, an Eclipse, owned by L. E. Slusser of Mancelona. The Eclipse engine was designed by Brownlow Starbuck of Mancelona. The September 27, 1906, *Mancelona Herald* reported, "Five prominent gentlemen drove an automobile to Bellaire in 55 minutes Saturday morning." The group of five—Judge Slusser, Dr. Beaver, Deputy Sheriff Kittle, Brownlow Starbuck, and the *Herald* editor—made good time, covering 12.5 miles.

Samuel Brockway, proprietor of the local island park located on Intermediate Lake north of Bellaire, was known as "Uncle Sam." Launches from Bellaire to the island maintained a regular schedule on weekends. The genesis of the park is not known, but in 1896, Uncle Sam began charging entrance fees—10¢ a head and 5¢ for children—to cover the cost of maintaining the park.

Uncle Sam's island park provided grounds for picnics, camping, and fishing and had a dance hall. Because the island was dependent on the water level in the lake, Uncle Sam had to occasionally remind the village to dredge the river. In 1906, however, when the Charlevoix Light Plant Dam was finished, the island park was under water. Samuel Brockway filed a lawsuit to cover his loss. In 1910, he lost the case; it seems he had never filed for ownership of the island.

In the photograph above, the Charles Wilcox and Charles May families wait on the dock for the boat to take them back from Uncle Sam's island park to Bellaire in 1899. The children seated on the dock are Charles Marshall May and Fern Wilcox, and on the far left stands Norma May. Other members of the families are not identified. The photograph below shows a typical picnic group at the island park during a time when one dressed up to go out—even a picnic required a hat. The members of this picnic are not identified.

In 1906, Samuel Brockway invited his GAR comrades to hold their 10th meeting on the island. Capt. Milton Kennedy conducted the meeting, Arch Cameron of Central Lake was elected chairman, and Dr. Bert C. Sickles of Bellaire was secretary. The group resolved to rename the island Logan's Island, as Maj. Gen. John A. Logan camped on the island during a fishing expedition in 1873. The general from Illinois commanded Michigan troops at Vicksburg and Atlanta during the Civil War. The resolution was accepted on November 17, 1906, with a copperplate engraving featuring General Logan's image for use on the new letterhead.

"Logan's Island," Dedicated Aug. 10, 1906 by Veteran Soldiers of 1861-5. Approved by Mrs. John A. Logan Nov. 17, 1906.

This photograph of Lake Bellaire looking to the northwest shows M-88, a north-south highway, and the road (west) to the lake. This road was built in 1890 when S. R. Large was paid $100 for the land. At the base of the hill was the Bellaire Brickyard. Horace L. Richards and Eugene Muckey leased the clay banks from S. R. Large. This brickyard supplied the yellow brick that was used to construct several buildings in Bellaire.

Visit us at
arcadiapublishing.com

www.ingramcontent.com/pod-product-compliance
Lightning Source LLC
Chambersburg PA
CBHW080558110426
42813CB00006B/1339